FORUNE'S

PASSIVE INCOME

BLUEPRINT

The Ultimate Guide to Making Money Even In Your Sleep

MAX FORTUNE

TABLE OF CONTENT

INTRODUCTION

PART ONE

Chapter ONE

UNDERSTANDING PASSIVE INCOME

What does Passive Income mean?

The Advantages of Passive Income

Different Passive Income Stream Types

Setting Financial Objectives for Passive Income

Dispelling frequently held myths and misconceptions

Assessing Your Present Financial Situation

The Success Formula for Passive Income

The Dangers and Difficulties of Passive Income

Taxes and Passive Income

A Passive Income Earner's Mentality

PART TWO

Chapter TWO

FINDING PROFITABLE PASSIVE INCOME OPPORTUNITIES

Researching Real Estate Investments

Examining Stocks That Pay Dividends

Producing and Marketing Digital Goods

Taking Advantage of Affiliate Marketing's Potential

High-Yield Bond Investing and Peer-to-Peer Lending

Utilizing Royalties and Licensing

Establishing and Funding a Website or Blog

Examining Rental Business Models

Understanding Automated Business Systems

Assessing the Potential of Franchising and Licensing

PART THREE

Chapter THREE

THE STEP-BY-STEP GUIDE TO GROWING PASSIVE INCOME

CONCLUSION

DISCLAIMER

INTRODUCTION

Thank you for visiting 'Fortune's Passive Income Blueprint: The Ultimate Guide to Making Money Even in Your Sleep.' Are you ready to discover the keys to financial independence and create a life of abundance? This book is your road map to generating various streams of passive income that work for you while you sleep. Prepare to learn strong tactics, real-life examples, and practical advice for making your aspirations a reality. Let's go on this road together and use the power of passive income to earn your wealth!

PART ONE

Chapter ONE

UNDERSTANDING PASSIVE INCOME

What does Passive Income mean?

Money produced with little to no direct work from the person receiving it is referred to as Passive Income. Unlike active income, which necessitates active participation in employment or services, Passive Income enables you to earn money while you're dozing off.

It comes from investments in businesses where you're not actively involved, such as rental properties, dividend-paying stocks, web ventures, and other working assets for you.

Since Passive Income is not reliant on exchanging labor for money, it offers some level of financial security and freedom.

Instead, it gives the opportunity to establish a long-lasting income stream that, once established, requires little ongoing work.

To fully appreciate the potential of Passive Income in obtaining financial independence, it is essential to understand the difference between active and Passive Income.

The Advantages of Passive Income

The advantages of Passive Income are numerous and can significantly affect your financial situation and way of life. Some of the main benefits are as follows:

1. Financial freedom: Passive Income offers a second source of income that is not reliant on exchanging time for money. It enables you to pay off debts, cover costs, and save and invest money for the future, which might result in financial freedom.

2. Diversification: It can be dangerous to simply rely on active income from one employment or source.

Your financial vulnerability to loss of employment or economic downturns is reduced by Passive Income, which diversifies your income sources.

3. Flexibility and Time Freedom: Having Passive Income gives you the freedom to work when you want and on your own terms. This enables you to spend more time with your loved ones, engage in hobbies, go on vacation, or do other things that are important to you.

4. Wealth Creation: Successful Passive Income endeavors, like stock portfolios or real estate investments, have the potential to increase in value over time, helping to build wealth and ensure financial security.

5. Less Stress and Burnout: Cutting less on active income can help with financial stress and fatigue brought on by long workdays.

Passive Income acts as a safety net, releasing you from continual concerns about money so that you may concentrate on developing personally and professionally.

6. Residual Income: A few Passive Income streams, such as royalties or dividends, may offer residual income over time. Once they are established, they can keep making money with little continuing work.

7. Retirement Planning: Creating Passive Income streams might be a useful retirement planning technique. You can complement retirement funds and live comfortably in retirement by generating a steady cash flow.

8. Scalability: Many Passive Income opportunities allow for scaling, which allows you to develop your business and boost profits without dramatically increasing your time commitment.

9. Location Independence: If you have access to the internet, Passive Income can give you the freedom to work from any location in the globe.

10. Personal Growth and Learning: Managing and developing passive revenue streams frequently requires acquiring new skills and accumulating worthwhile experiences. This personal development can be rewarding and aid in career advancement.

11. Generational Wealth: Some Passive Income assets, such as real estate, can be passed on to next generations, leaving a legacy of wealth for your family.

12. Empowerment and Control: Creating Passive Income enables you to take charge of your financial future and become less dependent on other factors. You gain the ability to control your financial future.

In general, Passive Income has several advantages besides financial ones. It gives you the independence and flexibility to create a life that is consistent with your objectives, principles, and desires.

However, it's crucial to remember that creating Passive Income frequently demands work and a financial commitment up front, but the benefits can be well worth the effort over time.

Different Passive Income Stream Types

Passive Income can be derived from a number of sources, each of which has distinct qualities and the potential to be profitable:

1. Real Estate: Real estate investments give you the chance to generate Passive Income by receiving rent payments from renters. Gains in real estate values can also add to long-term wealth.

2. Dividend-Paying Stocks: By distributing their profits to shareholders, companies that pay dividends can offer shareholders a steady stream of Passive Income.

3. Digital Products: Digital products and online businesses can produce Passive Income once the initial creation and promotion are complete. Examples include e-books, online courses, and software.

4. Affiliate Marketing: By using affiliate links to promote the goods or services of other people, you can make money from the purchases that result from your recommendations.

5. Peer-to-peer Lending: Platforms can generate interest income as borrowers pay back their loans by facilitating lending to people or businesses.

Setting Financial Objectives for Passive Income

Prior to starting your road toward Passive Income, it's crucial to establish definite and practical financial objectives. Establish your goals for Passive Income generation, including the amount and deadline.

Take into account your costs, financial condition, and any debts you intend to pay off.

Your Passive Income plan will have a clear road map if you set specified, measurable, attainable, relevant, and time-bound (SMART) targets.

Setting financial objectives for Passive Income is essential for laying out a clear path to obtaining your desired level of financial freedom. Here are some of the top methods for creating realistic financial objectives for Passive Income:

1. Be precise and measurable in your first step. Establish definite and defined financial objectives for your Passive Income. Give an example of how much passive revenue you wish to produce monthly or annually.

Measurable objectives enable you to monitor your progress and maintain motivation.

2. Align with your ideals and aims: Your financial objectives ought to be in line with your long-term aims and ideals.

Think on what you want to do with your Passive Income, whether it's an early retirement, a global tour, or funding a cause you care deeply about.

3. Set Achievable and Realistic Goals: Be honest with yourself about what you can accomplish with your Passive Income endeavors. Setting difficult-to-attain, excessively ambitious goals can cause discouragement and demotivation. Start with attainable benchmarks and change as you develop knowledge and assurance.

4. Time-Bound Goals: Give your financial objectives a deadline. Choose a time frame for achieving them, such as one year, five years, or ten years. Setting deadlines for your goals instills a sense of urgency and keeps you motivated to take constant action.

5. Divide bigger goals into smaller milestones: If your ultimate goal is big, divide it into smaller, more attainable milestones.

Celebrating each accomplishment will make you feel proud of yourself and inspire you to reach the next one.

6. Take into account the risks and sources of Passive Income: Various forms of Passive Income could have varied risks and returns. When establishing your financial goals, take into account any possible hazards related to each income source. To balance risk, diversification might be a wise strategy.

7. Review and revise regularly: You shouldn't have rigid financial objectives. Market conditions and life circumstances are subject to change. Review your objectives and progress on a regular basis, and be willing to make changes as necessary.

8. Have a specific action plan. Describe the steps you must take to achieve your objectives for Passive Income.

Set a timetable for the implementation of the specific investments, ventures, or assets you intend to pursue.

9. Seek professional advice: If you're unfamiliar with Passive Income or unclear of your goals, think about consulting with financial advisors or subject-matter specialists. They can offer insightful information and support you in making wise choices.

10. Maintain your commitment and discipline: Financial goals for Passive Income must be attained with dedication and self-control. Keep your goals in mind, stay away from distractions, and continually seek to expand your passive income sources.

11. Track and monitor progress: Keep track of your passive income profits and keep an eye on the success of your assets. Determine how near you are to accomplishing your goals on a regular basis and adapt as necessary.

You'll be better prepared to build a profitable and long-lasting portfolio of Passive Income that is in line with your entire financial plan and goals if you set clear and attainable financial goals for it.

Dispelling frequently held myths and misconceptions

While Passive Income is an appealing idea, it's important to dispel popular misunderstandings and misconceptions about it.

Some people think that Passive Income involves no effort at all, but in reality, it requires upfront work and continual maintenance. You can approach Passive Income with more realism and knowledge if you understand its true nature.

Myths about Passive Income include

1.   Passive Income requires no effort: A widespread misconception is that, once established, passive income streams require no effort.

In truth, the majority of Passive Income businesses need a large amount of upfront work, ongoing monitoring, and sporadic tweaks to maintain and function at their best.

2. Get rich quick with Passive Income: While passive income can be a helpful complement to your financial portfolio, attaining significant returns frequently needs time, patience, and constant work.

3.   Passive Income is always passive: Passive Income may not always be 100 percent passive. Some Passive Income sources, such as real estate investments or operating an online business, could necessitate sporadic engagement, decision-making, or customer service.

4. Passive Income is risk-free: Another myth is that Passive Income initiatives are risk-free. All investments and business endeavors have inherent dangers, therefore it's important to do your research and due diligence before deciding to invest in any Passive Income opportunity.

5. *Anyone can easily achieve Passive Income:* Although Passive Income is easily attainable, not everyone will succeed with it. A willingness to learn, adapt, and take calculated risks is necessary for creating and maintaining passive revenue sources.

6. *Passive Income is only for the wealthy:* Contrary to popular belief, there are many Passive Income alternatives that are appropriate for people from a variety of financial backgrounds and beginning places.

Dispelling Passive Income Myths and Misconceptions

1. Education and research: Inform yourself about Passive Income and the particular options you're interested in pursuing. To develop a genuine understanding of what Passive Income involves, do extensive research, read books, go to seminars, and get advice from knowledgeable people.

2. Realistic Expectations: Make sure your expectations for Passive Income enterprises are reasonable, both in terms of prospective returns and timelines.

Stay away from get-rich-quick schemes and concentrate on creating stable, long-term income streams instead.

3. Diversification: To disperse risk and improve the likelihood of overall success, diversify your sources of Passive Income rather than putting all your eggs in one basket.

4. Consistent work and monitoring: Despite the fact that Passive Income might gradually become less hands-on, it still takes work and monitoring. Dedicate time to managing your income streams, track their performance, and make required modifications.

5. Understand and manage risks: Recognize the risks involved in various Passive Income enterprises so that you may make educated selections and take the necessary precautions to reduce potential losses.

6. Focus on value creation: Stress giving value to your audience, clients, or customers rather to just concentrating on income providing high-quality goods, services, or content can result in devoted clients and ongoing Passive Income.

7. Continuous learning and adaptation: The world of Passive Income is continuously evolving, so staying curious and open to learning can help you stay ahead in your endeavors.

8. Getting Assistance: Consider getting assistance from professionals or mentors who have expertise in the Passive Income streams you're interested in pursuing. They can provide insightful advice based on their own experiences.

You may navigate the world of Passive Income more successfully and improve your prospects of reaching sustained financial success by dispelling myths and misconceptions about Passive Income and taking a realistic and informed approach.

Assessing Your Present Financial Situation

Conduct an in-depth analysis of your existing financial status to see whether your ambitions for Passive Income are realistic.

Determine your net worth, go over your sources of income and outgoing costs, and pinpoint the areas where Passive Income may have the biggest influence.

Knowing your financial situation can help you decide on Passive Income alternatives that will help you achieve your objectives.

The Success Formula for Passive Income

Starting with finding the Passive Income streams that resonate with your interests and align with your financial goals is the first step in developing a successful Passive Income plan. Research and evaluate each option's dangers and potential profits after that.

After choosing your streams, make a plan to put them up and take regular action to help them flourish and improve over time.

The Dangers and Difficulties of Passive Income

While Passive Income might be a tempting way to increase income and attain financial independence, it's important to be aware of and understand the risks and difficulties that come with this income strategy.

Some of the typical hazards and difficulties of Passive Income include:

1. Initial Investment Risk: Many Passive Income alternatives, such as real estate investing or beginning an online business, need an initial investment; nevertheless, there is a risk that the investment may not provide the anticipated returns or that it may take some time to break even.

2. Market Volatility: Passive Income streams connected to investments, such stocks or mutual funds, are prone to market volatility. Market fluctuations and economic downturns may have an effect on how these assets perform.

3. Fluctuations in income: Passive Income may not always be reliable. Some passive revenue sources, such as royalties or affiliate marketing, may see changes in profits depending on the state of the market, the actions of customers, or other circumstances.

4. Management and Maintenance: Some Passive Income sources, such as rental properties or web enterprises, necessitate constant management and maintenance. Tenant management, customer service, or updating digital items are some examples of this.

5. Liquidity Concerns: Other Passive Income assets, such as real estate or other investments, may have restricted liquidity, making it difficult to swiftly convert these assets into cash when needed.

6. Regulatory and Legal Risks: Regulatory or legal risks may be relevant, depending on the Passive Income possibility. Your Passive Income initiatives might be impacted, for instance, by tax restrictions, licensing needs, or intellectual property concerns.

7. Dependency on External Factors: Passive revenue streams frequently depend on uncontrollable external factors. The performance of your income sources may be affected by shifts in market trends, rivalry, or technological developments.

8. Scams and Fraud: Scammers and fraudulent schemes may be attracted by the attraction of Passive Income. To prevent falling for phony offers, it is essential to exercise caution and due care.

9. Time and Effort: Although Passive Income is intended to be less hands-on, setting up and maintaining income streams may involve a substantial amount of initial time and work. A strong Passive Income portfolio may require patience and persistent effort to develop.

10. Lack of Diversification: You run the risk of concentration if you rely too heavily on one source of Passive Income or asset. Spreading risk across a variety of Passive Income sources helps improve overall financial stability.

11. Competition and Saturation: Some Passive Income opportunities, such as affiliate marketing or online enterprises, may experience intense competition and saturation.

Innovative tactics could be needed to stand out and draw in a target audience.

12. Inflation Impact: It is critical to take inflation into account while defining financial objectives and choosing income streams because over time, inflation can reduce the purchasing power of Passive Income sources.

Despite these dangers and difficulties, Passive Income can still be a significant part of a comprehensive financial plan. Passive Income can make a major contribution to your financial security and long-term objectives with careful decision-making and continuing oversight.

Taxes and Passive Income

When creating and managing Passive Income streams, the relationship between Passive Income and taxes is a crucial factor to take into account.

Although Passive Income may have financial advantages, it is nonetheless subject to taxation like all other types of income.

To optimize your earnings and comply with tax rules, it's crucial to understand how taxes relate to Passive Income. Here are some important aspects to take into account:

1. Taxation of Passive Income Sources: Different Passive Income sources may be taxed in different ways. For instance:

- Rental income: Rental property income is typically taxable as income. Maintenance charges and property taxes are two examples of expenses relating to property management that may be deducted.

- Dividends: The income from stock dividends is sometimes taxed at a lower rate than income from regularly-occurring employment.

Non-qualified dividends are normally taxed at the individual's regular income tax rate, although qualified dividends may be taxed at a reduced rate.

- Interest is normally taxable as ordinary income when it is received through investments or savings accounts.

- Capital Gains: Capital gains tax may be owed on Passive Income derived from the sale of assets like stocks or real estate. Depending on the holding period and local tax regulations, the capital gains tax rate may change.

2. Tax Brackets and Passive Income: The amount of taxes you owe on your Passive Income can vary depending on your tax bracket. When combined with other income sources, Passive

Income has the potential to place you in a higher tax bracket and raise your entire tax obligation.

3. Tax-Efficient Investments: Investing in tax-efficient assets can assist reduce the impact of taxes on your Passive Income profits, since some Passive Income investments, such as tax-free municipal bonds, may offer tax advantages in certain locations.

4. Passive Losses and Passive Activities: Passive losses and passive activities can have complicated tax consequences.

In some circumstances, only Passive Income may be used to offset passive losses. Planning for taxes necessitates an understanding of the tax regulations governing passive losses.

5. Tax Credits and Deductions: Depending on the Passive Income activity, tax credits and deductions may be available. For instance, you can be eligible for certain tax credits if you invest in renewable energy projects.

6. Self-Employment Taxes: You may be liable for self-employment taxes in addition to income taxes if your Passive Income stems from endeavors in which you actively engage, such as operating an online business.

7. Reporting and Compliance: Keeping thorough records of income and expenses linked to your Passive Income enterprises is necessary for tax reporting purposes. It's crucial to accurately report your Passive Income and comply with tax rules.

8. Estate Taxes: These may apply when Passive Income assets are transferred to heirs or beneficiaries for estate planning reasons.

Given the difficulties in taxing Passive Income, it is best to speak with a tax expert or financial advisor to determine the precise tax ramifications of your Passive Income streams and to devise a tax-saving plan. Your Passive Income profits can be retained in greater amounts if you use effective tax planning, which can also help you avoid potential fines for non-compliance.

A Passive Income Earner's Mentality

A Passive Income earner's mindset is essential for success and financial independence through Passive Income sources.

A positive mindset can enable people to take charge of their financial future and make wise decisions.

Here are some fundamental components of a Passive Income earner's mindset:

1. Long-term perspective: A Passive Income earner has a long-term perspective, is willing to invest in assets and ventures that may not yield immediate returns but have the potential for steady growth over time, and understands that creating sustainable Passive Income streams requires time and patience.

2. Financial Education: Passive Income earners prioritize financial education and continually seek to expand their knowledge about various Passive Income opportunities, investment strategies, and wealth-building principles.

3. Entrepreneurial Spirit: For those who earn Passive Income, having an entrepreneurial spirit is essential. They are willing to investigate new possibilities, take reasonable risks, and adjust to market fluctuations.

This way of thinking promotes creativity and innovation when it comes to locating and creating Passive Income streams.

4. Risk Management: Successful Passive Income producers put a lot of emphasis on risk control. They recognize that there are risks associated with all investments and business initiatives and take precautions to diversify their income sources, thoroughly investigate new business prospects, and make well-informed judgments to reduce risks.

5. Consistency and Discipline: Passive Income producers value consistency and discipline in their behavior. They are devoted to taking constant action to develop and increase their Passive Income streams.

This may entail devoting time each week to their endeavors, watching their investments, or maintaining their Passive Income sources.

6. Focus on Value Creation: Passive Income earners prioritize adding value to their customers, clients, or audience because they know that satisfying others' needs and providing valuable goods, services, or content are the foundation of long-term Passive Income.

7. Ability to Adjust Strategies: Explore new income Streams, and Learn from Failures: Market conditions and opportunities can change, and Passive Income earners are adaptive and resilient in the face of adversities.

8. Patience: Building Passive Income streams may not give instant gratification, but Passive Income earners are patient and ready to put off current consumption in order to reap long-term financial benefits.

9. Goal-Oriented: Passive Income earners create specific, attainable financial goals, break down their objectives into manageable chunks, and celebrate accomplishments along the way, which keeps them inspired and focused on their path.

10. Financial Independence Mindset: Earners of Passive Income prioritize financial independence and are motivated to acquire financial freedom. They view Passive Income as a way to take back control of their finances, lessen financial stress, and enjoy life on their own terms.

It takes time to develop the mindset of a Passive Income earner, which calls for self-awareness, continuing learning, and a commitment to taking action. Individuals can lay a strong foundation for developing a successful portfolio of Passive Income streams by implementing these ideas.

You'll be well-prepared to start your quest to build sustainable and satisfying Passive Income streams if you comprehend the principles of Passive Income, recognize its potential benefits, and prepare for the challenges ahead.

PART TWO

Chapter TWO

FINDING PROFITABLE PASSIVE INCOME OPPORTUNITIES

Researching Real Estate Investments

Careful study and due diligence are needed when researching real estate investments in order to find lucrative opportunities and reduce dangers. Here is a step-by-step tutorial on conducting real estate investment research:

1. Specify your investment objectives: Establish your time horizon, risk tolerance, and financial goals. Choose whether you're looking for long-term growth, rental income, or both. The kind of real estate investment that best meets your objectives will depend on them.

2. Research the housing market: Investigate the area's real estate market before making an investment.

Examine the vacancy rates, rental demand, property price movements, and economic factors. Look for growth-oriented places where the real estate market complements your investing goals.

3. Recognize the several types of real estate: Learn about the different types of real estate, such as residential, commercial, industrial, and mixed-use buildings. Each category has different potential rewards and risks. When selecting a property type, take your tastes and experience into account.

4. Examine comparable rental and sales rates: In order to comprehend market values and pricing patterns, look into recent similar property sales. To determine possible rental income, look out the rental prices for nearby properties that are similar to yours. You can use this information to assess the potential for the property to generate income.

5. Examine the property and neighboring area: Perform a complete physical assessment of the property to spot any structural problems, maintenance requirements, or required repairs. Examine the neighborhood's amenities, accessibility to important services, schools, transit, and possibilities for future growth.

6. Assess cash flow and costs: Subtract costs (such as a mortgage, property taxes, insurance, and upkeep) from the rental income to determine the prospective cash flow of the property. Make sure there is enough cash flow to meet operating expenses and offer a return on investment.

7. Evaluate your financing options: Investigate all of your potential financing choices, including conventional mortgages, private lenders, and real estate investment partnerships. Examine how your overall investing strategy will be affected by financing, interest rates, and loan terms.

8. Reviewing legal and regulatory considerations is step eight: Do some homework on the zoning laws, property taxes, and any other legal constraints that might apply to the property. To manage any legal complications and guarantee compliance, consult with legal experts and real estate agents.

9. Take market liquidity and exit strategy into account: Examine the local real estate market's liquidity. If you need to get out of the investment, selling on a liquid market makes it simpler. Whether you plan to hold the investment for a long time, sell it, or reinvest the proceeds, have a clear exit strategy in mind.

10. Seek expert advice: Speak with knowledgeable local real estate brokers, property managers, or investors. Your ability to make wise decisions will be aided by their knowledge and insights.

11. Conduct a risk assessment: Examine possible investment risks, such as economic downturns, modifications to local laws, or tenant vacancies. Create backup plans to take care of these risks and protect your investment.

You'll be prepared to make wise real estate investment decisions by following these guidelines and completing in-depth research, positioning yourself for a fruitful and lucrative endeavor.

Examining Stocks That Pay Dividends

Investigating dividend-paying stocks entails performing analysis and research to find good investing prospects. Following are four methods to research dividend-paying stocks:

1. Stock screeners and financial websites: Use stock screeners and financial websites to filter and locate dividend-paying stocks according to predetermined parameters.

You can customize these platforms by choosing variables like dividend yield, dividend growth rate, market capitalization, and sector of industry.

Frequently visited financial websites like Yahoo Finance, Google Finance, or specialized stock screeners offer thorough information and stock research tools.

2. Lists of dividend achievers and aristocrats: Look at the Dividend Achievers and Dividend Aristocrats lists. The S&P 500 firms known as Dividend Aristocrats have grown their dividend payments for at least 25 years running, demonstrating their stability and dedication to their shareholders.

On the other hand, companies that have a history of steadily increasing dividends but may not be included in the S&P 500 are known as Dividend Achievers. These lists can be used as a jumping off point to find trustworthy dividend-paying stocks.

3. Reports on stock analysis and research: Access stock research and analysis reports from trustworthy brokerage companies and financial institutions. These reports frequently offer in-depth analysis of the financial performance, future prospects, and dividend practices of the firms.

Take note of variables such as earnings per share, payout ratios, debt levels, and management's dedication to dividend payments.

4. Dividend-paying Mutual Funds and ETFs: Think about investing in mutual funds or exchange-traded funds (ETFs) that are dividend-focused. These funds combine the money of numerous participants to make investments in a variety of dividend-paying stocks.

For investors looking for diversification, dividend ETFs and mutual funds offer exposure to a wide selection of dividend equities across numerous industries.

When researching dividend-paying stocks, it's crucial to strike a balance between high dividend yields and other fundamental elements including the company's financial stability, potential for profits growth, and dividend sustainability. You can develop a strong dividend portfolio that is in line with your investment objectives by conducting comprehensive research and keeping up with market trends.

Producing and Marketing Digital Goods

Making money by producing and selling digital goods can be a viable way to earn Passive Income. Here are five strategies for producing and marketing digital goods:

1. E-books and Online Manuals: E-books or digital manuals on subjects you are informed or enthusiastic about should be written and published. E-books can be offered on sites like Amazon Kindle, Apple Books, or your own website, whether they are self-help, recipe, or how-to books.

2. Online Tutorials and Courses: By producing tutorials or online courses, you can impart your knowledge. These can be in textual or video form and can cover topics like marketing, coding, photography, or any other skill you are particularly good at. You may host and sell your courses to a global audience using platforms like Udemy, Teachable, and Skillshare.

3. Graphical Layouts and Templates: Create digital templates for a variety of uses if you are skilled in graphic design. This might apply to downloadable calendars, social media templates, résumé styles, or website themes. On creative markets like Etsy or Creative Market, sell these templates.

4. Software and Mobile Apps: Create and market software applications or mobile apps to address particular requirements or offer solutions to widespread issues. Depending on your level of technical proficiency, you could develop software for specialized markets or productivity solutions.

You may access a sizable customer base by using marketplaces like the App Store and Google Play.

5. Stock Pictures and Videos: If you are a photographer or videographer, you can make money by offering your high-quality work as stock content. For use in websites, marketing materials, and multimedia projects, stock photos and videos are in high demand. Send your work to stock photo companies like Getty Images, Shutterstock, or Adobe Stock.

Put your target market's needs first while developing and marketing digital products. Spend time marketing and promoting your items using email marketing, social media, and partnerships with bloggers or influencers. You may gradually grow sales by interacting with your clients, gathering their feedback, and always enhancing your offers.

Taking Advantage of Affiliate Marketing's Potential

Exploiting affiliate marketing's potential can be a fruitful approach to generate passive revenue. These are three efficient strategies for utilizing affiliate marketing:

1. Select the Best Affiliate Programs: Your success as an affiliate marketer depends on choosing the appropriate affiliate programs. Look for shows that fit your niche or your target audience's interests. Select trustworthy affiliate networks or individual affiliate programs that provide fair commission rates, dependable tracking systems, and an extensive selection of high-quality goods or services to promote.

ClickBank, ShareASale, and Amazon Associates are a few well-known affiliate networks.

2. Produce Top-Notch Content and Establish Credibility: A potent tool for affiliate marketers is content marketing.

Create meaningful and high-quality material for your audience, such as blog entries, product reviews, how-to videos, or social media posts.

Concentrate on addressing issues, responding to inquiries, and emphasizing the advantages of the items you advocate.

Building audience trust is crucial because people are more inclined to follow your advice if they perceive you as a reliable authority in your market.

3. Diversify Your Channels for Advertising: To reach a larger audience and optimize your affiliate marketing potential, investigate several promotion platforms. Consider using social media channels, email marketing, YouTube, podcasts, and webinars in addition to your blog or website to advertise affiliate products. Every platform provides distinct chances to engage your audience and present your affiliate suggestions in various styles.

Your main objective should be to really assist your audience and solve their requirements, so be honest and steer clear of aggressive sales approaches.

Always follow the rules for affiliate marketing and be upfront about your affiliate agreements. By doing this, you may gain and keep your audience's trust. To maximize your affiliate revenue over time, keep a close eye on your affiliate performance, conduct data analysis, and modify your marketing tactics accordingly.

Affiliate marketing can develop into a dependable source of Passive Income with commitment, perseverance, and a focus on offering value.

High-Yield Bond Investing and Peer-to-Peer Lending

Peer-to-peer lending and investing in high-yield bonds can both present appealing options for producing Passive Income. Here are three key strategies for approaching these investment opportunities:

1. Research and Careful Consideration:

Do your homework and due diligence before investing in high-yield bonds or using a peer-to-peer lending platform.

Examine the financial stability, credit standing, and track record of the issuing corporation in the case of high-yield bonds. Recognize the risks involved with high-yield bonds because they frequently have higher default risks than investment-grade bonds. To disperse risk among several issuers and sectors, diversify your bond portfolio.

Examine the conditions, charges, and default rates of the lending platform in detail for peer-to-peer lending.

Examine the borrower selection procedure and the platform's history of default handling. Spread out your loans among a variety of debtors to lessen the impact of any defaults.

2. Evaluate the Return and Risk Profile:

Peer-to-peer lending and high-yield bonds both have the potential to generate greater returns than more conventional investments like savings accounts or government bonds. They do, however, carry greater hazards.

Before committing cash to these alternatives, it's critical to evaluate your risk appetite and investing objectives.

High-yield bonds could provide appealing returns, but they are more susceptible to fluctuations in interest rates and the state of the economy. Recognize how changing interest rates may affect the price of bonds, and be ready for possible price volatility.

Consider the risk-reward trade-off for different loan kinds and borrower profiles when it comes to peer-to-peer lending. Therefore, carefully balance the possibility of greater income against the danger of borrower defaults. Higher returns may be connected with higher default rates.

3. Portfolio Management and Risk Allocation:

Consider risk management and diversification while adding high-yield bonds and peer-to-peer lending to your investing portfolio. To establish a well-balanced and varied mix, these assets should complement your other holdings in your portfolio. You run the danger of concentration if you devote a sizable percentage of your portfolio to high-yield bonds or peer-to-peer lending. To spread risk and lessen the effect of unfavorable market circumstances on your total portfolio, balance your investments with other assets like stocks, real estate, and cash.

To preserve your preferred asset allocation, you should also examine and rebalance your portfolio on a regular basis. High-yield bonds and peer-to-peer lending performance can be impacted by market conditions and interest rate changes, so modifications may be required to meet your long-term financial objectives.

You can possibly profit from high-yield bonds' and peer-to-peer lending's potential to provide income while successfully managing associated risks if you approach them with rigorous research, risk assessment, and portfolio management.

Utilizing Royalties and Licensing

Royalties are sums of money given to the inventor or owner of intellectual property in exchange for their use or exploitation by another party.

The kind and sum of royalties can change based on the particular application of intellectual property. Here are the various royalties for various aspects:

1. Music royalties

When music is duplicated or circulated, such as when CDs or digital downloads are sold, songwriters and composers are compensated with mechanical royalties.

i. Performance royalties: These fees are given to the authors and publishers of songs when they are played publicly, whether live or via broadcast, streaming, or in open spaces like cafes or stores.

ii. Synchronization (Sync) Royalties: Sums paid to composers and music publishers for the inclusion of their songs in motion pictures, television programs, advertising, video games, and other forms of multi-media.

2. Book royalties

i. Print Book Royalties: Amounts given to authors for each print edition of their books that is sold.

ii. E-book Royalties: Amounts given to authors for each e-book or audiobook version of their publications that is sold. Authors are compensated with translation royalties when their books are translated and published in other languages.

3. Film and television royalties

i. Box Office Royalties: Amounts paid to movie producers and studios based on how well the picture performs at the box office.

ii. Home Video Royalties: Reimbursed for the sale or rental of movies and TV series on DVD and Blu-ray.

iii. Broadcast and Streaming Royalties: Paid when movies and TV shows are broadcast or streamed on television or online.

4. Software Royalties

i. Licensing Royalties: Sums paid to software developers in exchange for consumers' or organizations' use of their products. One-time payments or continuing subscription-based arrangements are also possible for licensing costs.

ii. Reseller Royalties: These fees are given to developers when independent resellers sell their software.

5. Patent Royalties: - Licensing Royalties: Paid to patent owners when other businesses or individuals make or market products using their patented technology. Licensing contracts may include a fixed price or a portion of revenues.

6. Licensing Royalties, which are paid to trademark owners when other companies use their logos, brand names, or catchphrases on goods or services.

7. Art and Photography Royalties - Licensing Royalties: Reimbursed to artists and photographers when their works of art or images are exploited for commercial endeavors, such as in publications, promotional items, or products.

8. Franchise Royalties: These fees are paid by franchisees to franchisors in exchange for the right to use the franchisor's branding, business model, and support services.

The specifics of royalty agreements might vary greatly, therefore it's crucial to keep in mind that dialogue between the parties is necessary to decide on the kind, sum, and length of royalties paid for the use of intellectual property.

Utilizing royalties and licensing can be a profitable strategy to make Passive Income by commercializing your creative works, intellectual property, or company ideas. Here are some tips for maximizing royalties and licensing:

2. Protecting your intellectual property is important.

Protecting your intellectual property is vital before looking at royalties and licensing. Copyrights for literary works, musical compositions, and creative creations are examples of this, as are patents for new ideas or innovative technology, as well as trademarks for branding and logos.

By registering it, you can gain legal protection and maintain control over how it is used and distributed.

2. Locate Possible Licensing Opportunities

To find prospective licensing prospects, evaluate your ideas, business methods, or artistic works.

Take into account the industries or enterprises that could profit from the usage of your intellectual property as well as the market demand for it. In order to provide value for customers, look for supplementary goods or services that might incorporate your intellectual property.

3. Recognize Licensing Agreements:

Create licensing agreements that specify the terms and conditions for using your intellectual property after you have identified possible licensing partners. The scope of use, length, royalty rates, and any limitations on its application should all be specified in the agreement. Consult with legal experts with knowledge of intellectual property to make sure the contract safeguards your interests and complies with the law.

4. Discuss Royalty Rates:

A crucial part of licensing agreements is negotiating royalty rates. The royalty rate is the portion of money that the licensee—the person who uses your intellectual property—will give you in return for allowing them to do so. Establish fair and reasonable royalty rates that are in line with industry norms and take into account the value that your intellectual property adds to the licensee's goods or services.

5. Observe and Enforce Compliance:

It's important to keep an eye on whether the licensing agreement is being followed while your intellectual property is licensed. To guarantee correct royalty payments, regularly analyze sales figures and financial statements from licensees. Put in place controls to ensure adherence and deal with any violations or unlawful use of your intellectual property.

6. Look for International Licensing Opportunities:

To increase your intellectual property's visibility and earning potential, look into overseas licensing alternatives. Creating partnerships with multinational corporations or looking for licensing deals in international marketplaces might provide new income streams and raise your royalty payments.

7. Utilize several licensing avenues:

Investigate several avenues to your fullest licensing potential. Consider licensing your music, for instance, if you're a musician, so that it can be used in movies, commercials, video games, or internet venues. If you have a patented innovation, look into licensing prospects with other businesses that could use it.

8. Work with agents and organizations:

Think about dealing with licensing agents or organizations with management experience for intellectual property rights.

To free you up to concentrate on your creative efforts or business, these experts may assist you in finding suitable licensees, negotiating advantageous contracts, and handling administrative responsibilities.

Your original works or novel ideas can become Passive Income streams by utilizing royalties and licensing. To maximize your intellectual property's potential in multiple industries and marketplaces, make sure you are aware of its value, protect it legally, and form strategic alliances.

Establishing and Funding a Website or Blog

A blog or website can be built and made profitable as a great way to make passive income. Following are five quick ways to begin going:

1. Create High-Quality Content: Place an emphasis on writing articles that will be helpful to, interesting to, and relevant to your target audience. Create blog posts, articles, or multimedia content like podcasts or videos.

Readers will be drawn to and remain on your website because of the high quality of the material.

2. Utilize Affiliate Marketing: Sign up for affiliate programs relevant to your specialty and use affiliate links to advertise goods or services. You get paid a commission when your readers use these links to make purchases. Be open and honest about your affiliate relationships with your readership.

3. Display Advertising: Join advertising networks like Google AdSense and use their services to display pertinent ads on your website or blog. Based on ad impressions and clicks, you'll receive payment. But be careful not to over-advertise your website, as this can ruin the user experience.

Create and market digital items like e-books, online courses, templates, or consulting services that are connected to your area of expertise.

4. Digital goods can offer a reliable source of income and have little overhead costs.

5. Create an Email List: Encourage website visitors to join your email list. Send your subscribers helpful updates and articles on a regular basis, and on occasion, advertise your own goods or affiliate deals. To foster relationships and increase sales, email marketing might be useful.

Keep in mind that creating and earning money from a blog or website requires time and effort. Put your attention on providing value to your readers and cultivating a following. Investigate additional monetization strategies as your website expands that fit your audience's tastes and niche.

To maximize the passive revenue you can generate from your blog or website, have an open mind to trying and improving your strategies.

Examining Rental Business Models

Entrepreneurs might explore a variety of rental company strategies to create Passive Income.

Each strategy entails renting out items or offering clients services in exchange for a price. Here are some various rental business concepts and information on how to investigate them:

1. Residential Property Rentals: Start by buying or renting residential properties, including condos, homes, or apartments, and then renting them to renters. Investigate the rental market, demand for rentals, and prospective rental income in various neighborhoods. To measure profitability, total costs such as the mortgage, maintenance, insurance, and property taxes.

2. Renting out Commercial Property: Think about renting out or owning commercial assets, including office buildings, retail storefronts, or industrial warehouses, to businesses. Analyze the prospective demand from nearby firms and determine whether commercial rental properties are economically viable.

3. Equipment Rentals: - Investigate by buying machinery, tools, or equipment and renting them to organizations or people. Make sure that the necessary upkeep and safety precautions are in place when researching the need for a specific piece of equipment in your target market.

4. Car Rentals: Take into account beginning a business where you provide customers short-term rentals of your vehicles. Look into the local rental vehicle market, evaluate the competitors, and think about collaborating with hotels or travel companies to reach more people.

5. Vacation Rentals: Investigate the vacation rental market by making homes or rooms available to tourists for short-term leases. Utilize websites like Airbnb or VRBO to promote your holiday rentals and draw visitors.

6. Event Rentals: - Take into account offering rental services for occasions like weddings, parties, or business gatherings. Rent out furniture such as tents, seats, tables, and decorations. Make connections with venues and event organizers to look into possible collaborations.

7. Storage Space Rentals: Start by renting out storage space to people and corporations. Self-storage facilities or warehouse areas may be included. Determine the demand for storage in your area and make sure the rental spaces have suitable security.

8. Boat or RV Rentals: Take into account providing boat or RV rentals to people or families seeking for leisure activities.

Consider working with marinas or RV parks after researching how popular boating or RVing is in your area. Conduct market research to assess the demand and competition in your chosen location before exploring various rental business options.

Analyze the prospective expenses and money generated by each model, including the price of purchase or lease, ongoing costs, and potential rental income.

Create a strong business strategy that details your rental services, marketing plans, costs, and customer service philosophy.

Comply with local laws and secure any licenses or permissions required for your rental business. Your success in the rental market will be aided by providing exceptional customer service and maintaining the caliber of your rental properties.

Understanding Automated Business Systems

Automated business systems are procedures or workflows that require little to no manual involvement to function, eliminating the need for ongoing supervision and management. These techniques are used to generate cash with little continuing work, hence creating Passive Income streams.

Here are a few instances of automated business systems and how to turn them into sources of Passive Income:

1. Dropshipping: With the dropshipping business concept, you may offer things to customers online without maintaining an inventory.

The product is transported straight from the supplier to the customer once a customer puts an order. Automate order processing and combine it with suppliers and shipping firms to turn dropshipping into a Passive Income generator.

To administer the store and automate customer interactions, use e-commerce platforms like Shopify or WooCommerce.

2. Print-on-Demand (POD): With print-on-demand, you can design things with a unique design, such as T-shirts, mugs, or phone cases, and have them manufactured and dispatched as soon as an order is placed. Partner with POD businesses that manage printing, fulfillment, and shipping to automate your print-on-demand business.

Integrate your online store with the POD platform to enable automatic order processing and delivery.

3. Websites for affiliate marketing: Create niche websites that are concentrated on a single subject or sector, then utilize affiliate marketing to monetise them. Publish top-notch content with affiliate connections to goods and services. For organic traffic, optimize your website for search engines.

As more people visit and trust your website, it may start to generate Passive Income from sales made by users who click on your affiliate links.

4. Online Courses and Membership Sites: - Create membership sites that provide exclusive content, lessons, or tools and develop and sell online courses.

To automate the delivery of courses and membership access, use systems like Teachable, Thinkific, or MemberPress.

Once the system is set up and the content is created, new enrollments can provide Passive Income without ongoing manual work.

5. Launch an online subscription box business where customers receive well picked products on a regular basis. Automate order processing, delivery, and subscription administration. To keep customers interested and to encourage subscription renewals, constantly source and curate new products.

6. Automated Email Marketing: Create campaigns for automated email marketing to interact with current and potential consumers. Use email sequences and autoresponders to send out follow-up emails, promotions, and other useful content. You may turn prospects into clients and create Passive Income from repeat business by nurturing leads and establishing relationships through automated emails.

Concentrate on initial setup, optimization, and continuing monitoring to make these automated business systems passive revenue producers. Spend time and energy developing valuable content, premium products, and successful marketing tactics.

To ensure that your systems produce the best outcomes and can react to shifting market trends, continuously evaluate and improve them.

It's crucial to keep in mind that even while automated solutions might considerably minimize manual labor, some amount of upkeep and supervision is still required. To keep your automated business profitable and productive, regularly check your systems, monitor performance indicators, and swiftly handle any problems or client enquiries.

Assessing the Potential of Franchising and Licensing

Analyzing the viability and advantages of these business expansion methods is a necessary step in evaluating the possibilities of licensing and franchising.

Both licensing and franchising enable business owners to expand the market for their ideas, goods, or services without having to operate directly. The potential for franchising and licensing can be assessed as follows:

1. Licensing: Evaluation of Your Intellectual Property: Find out if your company has distinctive intellectual property that can be licensed to others, such as patents, trademarks, copyrights, or trade secrets. You can license your intellectual property so that other businesses may use it in return for royalties or licensing costs.

i. Market Demand Analyze the demand in various markets or industries for your intellectual property. Think about what companies or sectors might gain from utilizing your technology, brand, or creative efforts.

ii. Profitability and Royalty Rates Analyze any possible financial gains from licensing. Estimate the possible revenue from licensing agreements by calculating the royalty rates or licensing fees you could impose.

iii. Protection and Control: Take into account how licensing your intellectual property might affect the reputation of your business and quality assurance. To protect your intellectual property and guarantee its legitimate usage, implement appropriate legal agreements and quality control methods.

2. Franchise opportunities - Replicability of business models Determine whether your business model can be successfully executed in several regions and is easily repeatable. Giving people the authority to use your brand and established business model is known as franchising.

i. Reliable Results: An established brand reputation and a track record of profitable operations are frequently necessary for successful franchising.

Consider whether your company has the potential for sustained success across many markets when you assess its performance.

ii. Franchisee Support: Think about the assistance and tools you can offer franchisees, such as continuous support, marketing, and training. Franchisees who receive sufficient support from the franchisor are more likely to be successful.

iii. Franchisee Choice: Create criteria for choosing franchisees who have the knowledge, means, and dedication to operate a successful franchise. The appropriate franchisees can help your franchise network succeed and expand.

3. Legal and Regulatory Considerations - Be aware of the licensing and franchising laws and regulations in your target areas. Consult with legal professionals to create thorough agreements that abide by all applicable laws and rules.

i. Be open and honest with prospective licensees and franchisees about the conditions, commitments, and expectations related to licensing or franchising your company.

4. The long-term plan is as follows: Think about how franchising or licensing would fit into your long-term business plan. Analyze each option's potential advantages and disadvantages, as well as how they relate to your growth goals.

You may decide whether these business expansion options are appropriate for your particular firm and market conditions by carefully assessing the possibility of licensing and franchising.

Both strategies can help you expand your company without needing to make big financial investments, but they both involve careful planning, legal considerations, and continuing support to be implemented successfully.

You'll learn more about a variety of lucrative Passive Income sources in Chapter 2. Each part will give you the information and resources you need to evaluate the possibility of various income streams and make decisions that are in line with your financial objectives and desires.

PART THREE

Chapter THREE

THE STEP-BY-STEP GUIDE TO GROWING PASSIVE INCOME

Congratulations! You've now looked into a number of potential sources of Passive Income. As you set out on your quest to create a reliable source of Passive Income, let's review the essential stages that will help you along the way:

Step 1: Establish Your Objectives for Passive Income

- Establish your financial goals, whether they are to save for retirement, become financially independent, or pay for a dream vacation.

- To stay motivated and focused on your financial goals, set precise and realistic Passive Income targets.

Step 2: Determine Your Areas of Expertise and Interests - Determine your strengths, interests, and specialties.

Making the most of what you already know and love might result in more fun and prosperous endeavors.

Step 3: Perform Market Research - Examine various Passive Income opportunities and their market viability.

- To make wise choices, consider trends, demand, and competition in your selected niche.

Step 4: Select the Appropriate Passive Income Streams

- Choose many income streams that fit your interests, abilities, and financial objectives.

- Your investments should be diversified to reduce risk and maximize rewards.

Step 5: Produce High-Quality Products and Content

- Concentrate on offering your audience or clients value through premium content, goods, or services.

- To gain credibility and trust, position yourself as an expert in your field.

Step 6: Establish and Use an Online Presence

- Establish a website, blog, or social media accounts to connect with more people.

- To increase traffic and revenues, use digital marketing techniques like SEO, email marketing, and social media advertising.

Step 7: Automate Business Processes - To reduce manual labor and save time, implement automated business solutions like dropshipping, print-on-demand, or online courses. Maintain regular system optimization and monitoring to ensure optimal effectiveness.

Step 8: Protect Your Intellectual Property - If necessary, get patents, copyrights, or trademarks to guard against unlawful use of your intellectual property.

- Investigate licensing alternatives to commercialize your IP and produce Passive Income.

Step 9: Diversify Your Investment Portfolio - To build a well-rounded investment portfolio, invest in a variety of assets such real estate, dividend-paying equities, bonds, and peer-to-peer lending.

- To optimize your Passive Income plan, balance risk and return.

Step 10: Monitor and Adjust - Constantly keep an eye on how your investments and Passive Income streams are doing.

- Based on changes in your financial goals, client input, and market trends, make adjustments.

Keep in mind that creating Passive Income requires patience, perseverance, and effort. Remain dedicated to your objectives and open to investigating new opportunities. Consider reinvesting some of the gains as your Passive Income increases to broaden your portfolio and hasten your path to financial freedom.

You'll be well on your way to gaining better financial stability and taking advantage of the advantages of financial independence by adhering to this step-by-step manual and being committed to your Passive Income endeavors. Wishing you success as you pursue Passive Income.

CONCLUSION

As we come to the end of 'Fortune's Passive Income Blueprint: The Ultimate Guide to Making Money In Your Sleep,' we hope you feel inspired and prepared to take control of your financial destiny. Remember that creating passive income is a journey that involves commitment and perseverance. Adopt the principles and strategies outlined in this book, and watch your wealth rise as you realize the actual potential of passive income. May your dreams come true, and may your riches flourish as a result of the passive income streams you've created. Here's to a prosperous and plentiful future!

www.ingramcontent.com/pod-product-compliance
Lightning Source LLC
Chambersburg PA
CBHW050749260726
48661CB00001B/495